AF480568

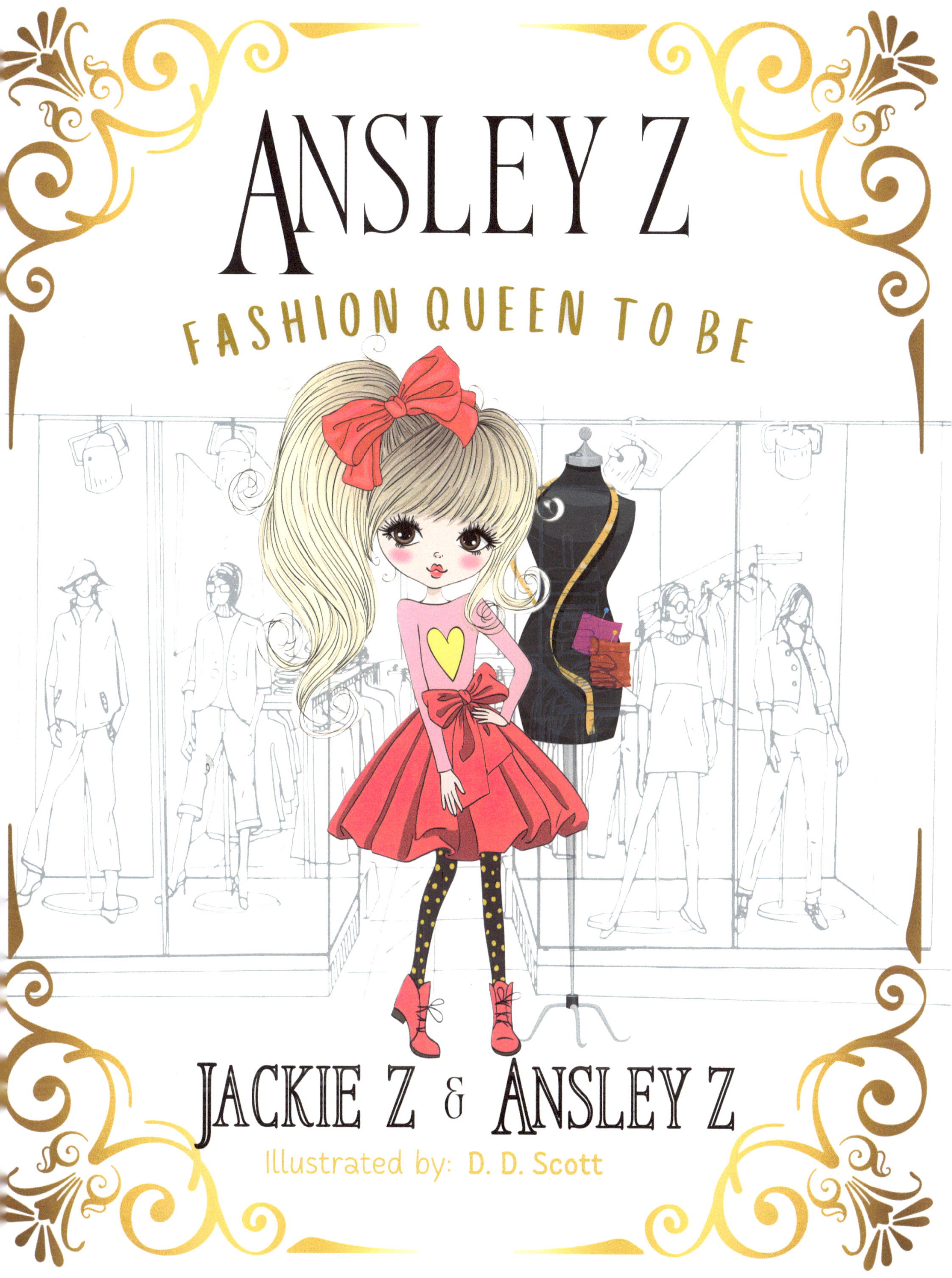

ANSLEY Z
FASHION QUEEN TO BE
Jackie Z & Ansley Z
Illustrated by: D. D. Scott

First Electronic Edition: December 2022

First Print Edition: December 2022

Illustrated by: D. D. Scott

This book is dedicated to the best husband and father in the world ~~ Brian Kins!

We love you to the moon and beyond.

You're our forever brightest star!

Love -- Jackie & Ansley

FASHION
STYLE

There once was a very special girl whose passion was all-things fashion. Her name was Ansley Z, and she was indeed a Fashion Queen to Be.

Her mom, Jackie Z, owned a store, where it was all about what men, women, and children wore.

At Jackie Z Style Company fashion reigned supreme, and Ansley Z could live out every single one of her wildest fashion dreams.

You see, Ansley Z was destined for greatness in the fashion world, by age 2, for example, she was on TV giving fashion shows her own unique swirl.

With her vibrant personality, there was nothing Ansley Z couldn't make or do, and by age 7, that included the incredible frocks she designed and drew.

She doodled clothing and purses, creating the most beautiful garments her mother had ever seen. Even their in-house master tailor agreed that she would someday be the next fashion queen.

He sought out the most beautiful fabrics from all over
the world to make her designs, and it wasn't long before
it was her fancy dresses that became Jackie Z customers'
latest obsessions.

"I love these!" Customer after customer exclaimed, buying up every single dress Ansley Z made.

That's when Jackie Z knew her daughter had a very special gift, one that was giving their customers quite the stylish uplift.

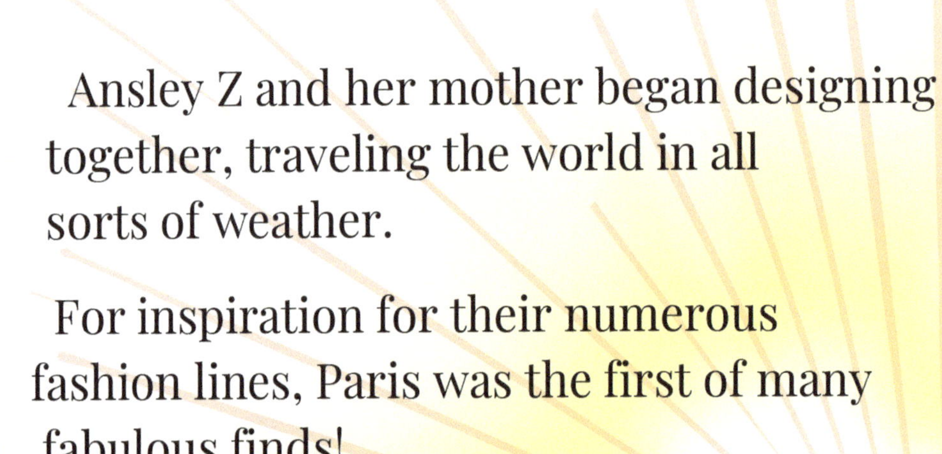

Ansley Z and her mother began designing together, traveling the world in all sorts of weather.

For inspiration for their numerous fashion lines, Paris was the first of many fabulous finds!

It was there they saw the finest frocks, by the likes of Chanel, Dior, and more, and they vowed to bring all that kind of fashion exquisiteness to their own fashion store.

Back at home, Ansley Z began drawing and cutting and sewing up a storm, bringing her designs to life as fashion's newest and brightest "norm".

In Australia, Ansley Z met all the famous social media stars, who helped her designs go viral. It wasn't long before the demand for her fashions would spiral.

But she was only 11 years old, and her mother wouldn't let her quit school. So, their passion for fashion had to come with a few rules.

Jackie Z would run her style company during the day, as well as help Ansley Z build her empire along the way.

They started to manufacture the goods themselves, in the good ol' US of A, even hiring local people to cut and sew, so as to stay, at least in part, handmade.

So there you have it, the story of a little girl
with fashion skills galore, a child with dreams
and hopes so big about what everyone wore.

But it wasn't that her high-fashion ways were
meant to be fickle, her magical frocks were
created to tickle. She was a fashionista, who
definitely, like her mother, dressed the part, but
Ansley Z was also nothing but heart.

She wanted to help people look and feel their best, and she would never ever settle for anything less.

The End
actually ...
it's just the beginning

FASHION
shion
trendy
CLASSY
hot beauty
STYLE
JACKIE Z style co.
JACKIE Z style co.
NOT
magazine
classy
fashion
BEAUTY
beauty
HO
P
pr
STYLE
posh
stylish
MODEL
hot
magazine
STYLE
fas
magazine
posh
trendy
star
not
JACKIE Z style co.
PURE
supermodel
Fashion
MODEL
dre
supermodel
FASHION
class
HOT
magazine
star
accessories
fashion
JACKIE Z

JACKIE Z

JACKIE Z (Jackie Zumba Kins) is the CEO of JZ Brands, Jackie Z Style Co & Zstacks. She's a Fashion Designer, Fashion Stylist, and a LifeStyle Guest on Daytime. She loves all things fashion, but mostly, she loves spending time with her family.

Step into her world at www.jackiezstyle.com

JACKIE Z

ANSLEY Z (Ansley Kins) is the
8-year-old daughter of
Brian and Jackie Kins. They live in
St. Petersburg, Florida. Ansley loves
dancing, gymnastics, cheerleading,
and of course, all-things fashion.

Books By The Authors

ANSLEY Z: FASHION QUEEN TO BE

MORE COMING SOON!

About the Illustrator

D. D. Scott is an International Bestselling Author, Illustrator, Writing & Publishing Coach, and Self-Publishing Strategist. With 47 books in 8 genres and over 1.4 million copies sold, she's been blessed to be an Amazon Top 10 Bestseller (multiple times) as well as a #1 Barnes & Noble bestseller. She is also the Founder and CEO of LetLoveGlow Author Services and 4everglow (a children's book co-op), where she lights the publishing path for hundreds of authors. Connect with her at www.LetLoveGlow.com